OGLETHORPE

Written and Illustrated
By
Katherine Yanez-Arellano

Order this book online at www.trafford.com
or email orders@trafford.com

Most Trafford titles are also available at major online book retailers.

 www.trafford.com

North America & international
toll-free: 1 888 232 4444 (USA & Canada)
fax: 812 355 4082

Our mission is to efficiently provide the world's finest, most comprehensive book publishing
service, enabling every author to experience success. To find out how to publish your book,
your way, and have it available worldwide, visit us online at www.trafford.com

Because of the dynamic nature of the Internet, any web addresses or links contained in this book may have changed
since publication and may no longer be valid. The views expressed in this work are solely those of the author and do
not necessarily reflect the views of the publisher, and the publisher hereby disclaims any responsibility for them.

Any people depicted in stock imagery provided by Getty Images are models,
and such images are being used for illustrative purposes only.
Certain stock imagery © Getty Images.

ISBN: 978-1-4907-9888-2 (sc)

ISBN: 978-1-4907-9887-5 (e)

Library of Congress Control Number: 2019921196

Print information available on the last page.

Trafford rev.03/06/2020

Dedicated to my Aunt Elizabeth

Prologue

James Edward Oglethorpe's high-minded idealism, combined with his fighting spirit, gave him the unique ability to establish the colony of Georgia and set into motion reforms that would greatly contribute to America's exceptionalism. Born into England's wealthy aristocracy on December 22, 1696, he grew up at Westbrook Manor, a large farming estate. Later, he would inherit Westbrook from his father, Sir Theophilus Oglethorpe, one of a long line of rugged military men who served the English Crown. This mantle would be passed down to his son, as well as his service in Parliament representing the county of Haslemere. Through his mother, Eleanor Wall Oglethorpe, James would meet leading writers and political thinkers of his day who discussed, among other things, humanitarian ideas like prison reform. In 1714, James entered Corpus Christi College, Oxford, but soon left to become aide-de-camp to Prince Eugene of Savoy during the Austro-Turkish War of 1716-18.

Oglethorpe was primed, so it would seem, to fulfill the role of the founder of Georgia. Consider the reasons for creating the 13th colony: number one, to provide a second chance for victims of debtors' prison; secondly, to create an agricultural enterprise for purposes of trade with England; and thirdly, to create a military zone between South Carolina and Spanish held Florida.

Correspondingly, Oglethorpe was motivated to become a big advocate of prison reform after discovering that his old school colleague, the architect, Robert Castell, had succumbed to smallpox in debtors' prison. He would also use Castel's book, "Villas of the Ancients," to lay out the beautiful city of Savannah on a grid interspersed with gardens.

Secondly, Oglethorpe was highly qualified to head an agricultural venture due to his having successfully managed the large farm at Westbrook Manor. He was particularly known for his bountiful grape vineyards. The colonist would experiment with olives, wines, silks, and flax.

Thirdly, Oglethorpe was an accomplished soldier. At age twenty, Oglethorpe had distinguished himself fighting in the Battle of Belgrade against the Turks. He would likewise find success at the Battle of Bloody Marsh fighting against the Spanish. In addition, he oversaw the construction of Ft. Frederica on St. Simons Island in order to protect the fledgling colony.

The "Oglethorpe" poem is a tribute to a man who used his position of privilege to give privileges to others. There will never be a utopia on Earth; however, through the lives of a few exceptional men, we can witness the needle moving in the direction of a far more fair and just society. One such exceptional man was the founder of Georgia, James Edward Oglethorpe.

May the vehement winds of Georgia forever rail against debtor's prison!

The sentiment wrought by Oglethorpe in his philanthropic vision.

May those westward winds guide the sails of Ann, velum of that valorous velero.

And with Oglethorpe's boldness…

Oglethorpe's boldness, sail up to that palmetto shore.

Unlock those dungeons of despair that reek of hopelessness!

Purge those smallpox infested caverns, oh! Westward winds of largesse!

For out of the hills of Haslemere a gallant aristocrat came,

And with Oglethorpe's benevolence…

Oglethorpe's benevolence, did undo those unjust chains.

James Edward Oglethorpe to Westbrook Manor was bore,

The seventh-son-of-seven-sons to Sir Theophilus and Lady Eleanor.

Did willingly sacrifice his personal wealth to give refuge to the poor.

And with Oglethorpe's succor…

Oglethorpe's succor, brought them to that magnificent shore.

Like thwarted twisted roots of Georgia's tenacious live oaks,

Those torpid tentacles did pierce the loam of Oglethorpe's Roanoke.

Like his predecessor, Raleigh, great obstacles he did encounter;

But with Oglethorpe's diligence…

Oglethorpe's diligence, his colony did not flounder.

Heat, mosquitoes and typhoid fever, many succumbed to the plague;

The first orphanage in Bethesda, Charles Whitefield's parishioners pledged.

The homeless, hard-working religious sects, by their own countries refused;

But with Oglethorpe's tolerance…

Oglethorpe's tolerance, gave refuge to both Protestants and Jews.

It was on that Savannah shore, those two like-souls did meet,

Oglethorpe and Chief Tomochichi, welding England with the Creeks.

Translated by aide, a proprietor of trade, that Scot-Indian maid, Mary Musgrove;

And with Oglethorpe's fairness…

Oglethorpe's sense of fairness, forged a bond over a buffalo robe.

On that robe-an eagle, foreshadowing with the forefathers' emblem,

Swiftly it flew from Coweta-to Buckingham Palace in England.

There a watch was given to Toonahowi, Tomochichi's adopted son.

And with Oglethorpe's diplomacy...

Oglethorpe's diplomacy, the first Native American school, Irene, was begun.

From the mulberry leaves to the silkworm's cocoon,

Silk! Fit for a king! From the Salzburgers' looms,

Was presented at court for Queen Caroline's dress.

And with Oglethorpe's finesse...

Oglethorpe's finesse, funds were raised with success!

King George, embroiled in a war with Spain, sent troops to construct Ft. Frederica,

And attack the Florida fort in St. Augustine constructed of coquina.

But with those catch-cannonball-walls, the mission looked disastrous,

But with Oglethorpe's cunning…

Oglethorpe's cunning, at Bloody Marsh he was victorious!

Hail! To Oglethorpe who was against rum, slavery, and lawyers.

(Though the founder would find it easier to keep gators out of Georgia.)

Hail! To the reformer, Oglethorpe. There are no debtors' prisons!

If not for Oglethorpe's idealism…

Oglethorpe's idealism, incarcerated we'd all be, indebted to his vision.

The Georgia Frontier

Cherokees

Upper
Creeks

Chattahoochee R.

Coweta Town
Cusseta

Lower
Creeks

Flint River

Apalachees

During the Oglethorpe Years

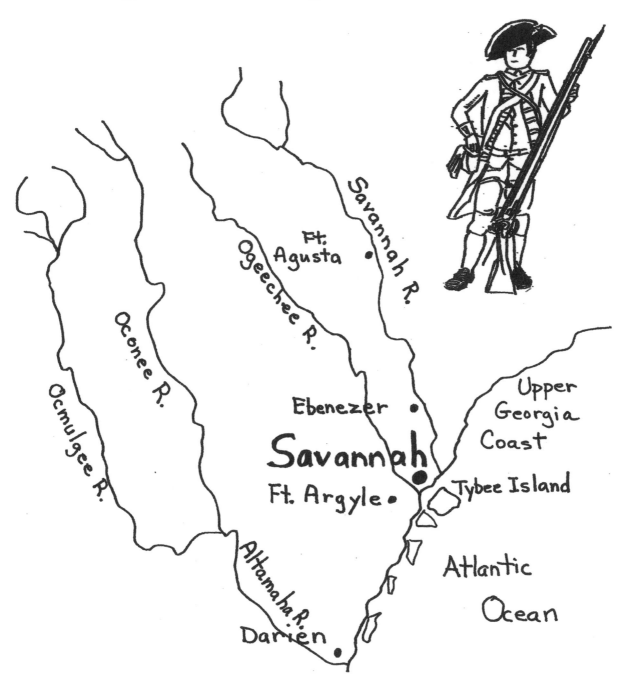

Savannah R.

Ft. Agusta

Ogeechee R.

Oconee R.

Ocmulgee R.

Ebenezer

Savannah

Ft. Argyle

Upper Georgia Coast

Tybee Island

Atlantic Ocean

Altamaha R.

Darien

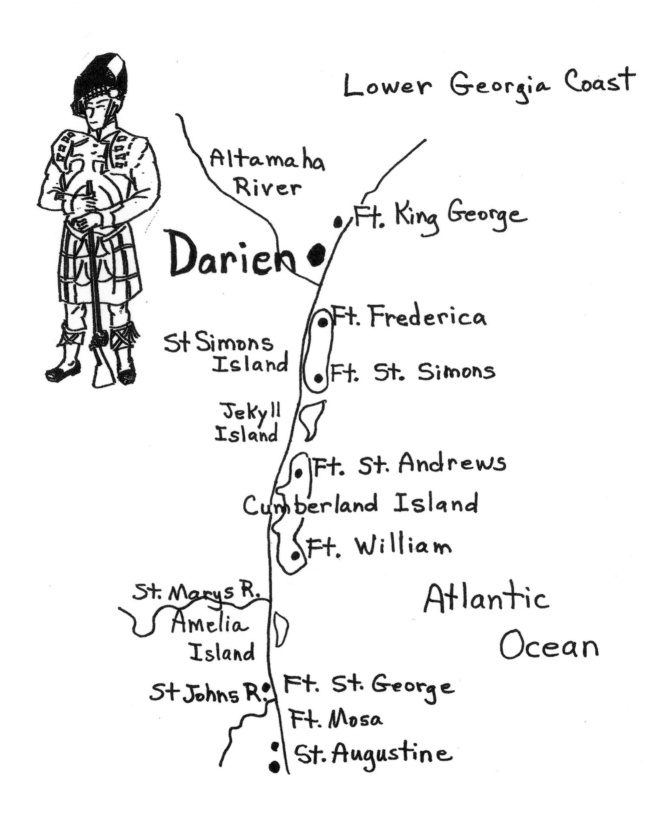

Lower Georgia Coast

Altamaha River

Ft. King George

Darien

Ft. Frederica

St Simons Island

Ft. St. Simons

Jekyll Island

Ft. St. Andrews

Cumberland Island

Ft. William

St. Marys R.

Atlantic

Amelia Island

Ocean

St Johns R.

Ft. St. George

Ft. Mosa

St. Augustine

Printed in the United States
By Bookmasters